# SHACKS, SHELTERS & SHANTY TOWNS ● BARACKEN, UNTERKÜNFTE & INFORMELLE SIEDLUNGEN
## CHOZAS, CHABOLAS Y RANCHERÍOS ● CABANES, ABRIS ET BIDONVILLES

● English ● Deutsch ● Español ● Français

With the migration of workers from rural settlements to the cities across South Africa, informal communities have been established on undeveloped land in closer proximity to towns and cities.

Resourceful residents have created makeshift homes and like a brightly woven patchwork quilt, as the shacks cover the dusty landscape, the earth comes to life with a surreal and gritty beauty.

A colourful sub-culture has sprung up from the streets of the townships – complete with its own township slang, vibrant art and informal industries like the outdoor hairdresser, the pavement fruit-seller, and the corner 'spaza' shop, and a bustling taxi fleet ferries workers to and from their place of work. Regardless of their circumstances, residents display a hopefulness that this Rainbow Nation will evolve to meet their needs, and those of all her people.

Überall in Südafrika wo Arbeitsuchende aus ländlichen Gebieten in die Städte zogen, sind auf unerschlossenem Land in der näheren Umgebung von Dörfern und Städten informelle Siedlungsgebiete entstanden.

Wo einfallsreiche Bewohner provisorische Unterkünfte errichtet haben und ihre Blech- und Bretterbuden wie ein leuchtender Fleckenteppich den staubigen Boden überziehen, wächst aus der Erde ein Landschaftsbild von surrealer und grobkörniger Schönheit.

Eine bunte Subkultur hat sich in den Straßen der Townships entfaltet – mit eigenem Township Slang, lebendigen Kunstformen, informellen Geschäftszweigen wie Freiluftfriseuren, Obst- und Gemüseständen, „Spaza"-Buden an der Straßenecke und einer Flottille von Taxis, die das Heer der Arbeitenden transportiert. Unter welchen Umständen auch immer, die Anwohner sind voller Hoffnung, dass diese Regenbogennation eines Tages ihre eigenen und die Bedürfnisse all ihrer Menschen erfüllen wird.

Con la migración de trabajadores de partes rurales a las ciudades a lo largo de Sudáfrica, se han establecido comunidades informales en terrenos urbanos y baldíos, alrededor de los pueblos y ciudades.

Residentes hábiles han creado hogares improvisados; como una colcha de retazos cubren el paisaje polvoriento dando vida a un paisaje surrealista y de marcado contraste.

Una subcultura vivaz ha salido de las calles de los barrios – con su propio jerga, arte vibrante e industrias informales como peluqueros al aire libre, vendedores de fruta sobre las veredas, y la "spaza" (tipo cafetería) en la esquina, y con un bullicioso flete de taxis transportando trabajadores de ida y vuelta a sus lugares de trabajo. A pesar de sus circunstancias, los habitantes manifiestan una ilusión de optimismo que ésta nación evolucionará para cumplir sus esperanzas y las de todo su pueblo.

Suite au déplacement de la population ouvrière des villages ruraux vers les villes à travers l'Afrique du Sud, des communautés informelles ont été établies sur des parcelles de terre non exploitée à proximité des villes.

Des résidents ingénieux y ont bâti des logements de fortune et, telle une couverture en patchwork de couleurs vives entrelacées, les cabanes recouvrent le paysage poussiéreux, animant la terre d'une beauté graveleuse et surréaliste.

Une subculture colorée s'est mise alors à proliférer des rues des townships, avec son propre argot dit des townships, son expression artistique dynamique et ses commerces informelles comme le salon de coiffure en plein air, le marchand de fruits installé sur le trottoir, le « spaza » du coin, sans oublier la flotte de taxis affairés à faire la navette, transportant les travailleurs entre leur domicile et leur lieu de travail. Peu importe leur situation, les habitants font preuve d'un espoir qui est celui que cette nation arc-en-ciel se développera afin de satisfaire à leurs besoins, ainsi qu'à ceux de tout son peuple.

● Homes are precariously built with salvaged pieces of cardboard, wood, corrugated iron and chipboard. Generous splashes of colour uplift them from these tawdry foundations. Enterprising residents use whatever has been abandoned, traded or donated to improve and enhance. A sense of self-worth is ever-present as can be seen in the freshly-washed garments that hang out in the humble backyard.

● Die Unterkünfte sind aus Resten von Pappe, Holz, Wellblech und Spanplatten notdürftig zusammengezimmert. Billigst aufgerichtet sind sie freigebig mit Farbe bekleckst, was ihnen ein gewisses äußeres Ansehen verleiht. Erfinderische Anwohner nutzen alles was weggeworfen, getauscht oder verschenkt wird zur Verbesserung ihrer Umstände. Die Menschen hier haben ein starkes Selbstwertgefühl, was an den frisch gewaschenen Kleidungsstücken zu erkennen ist, die in den bescheidenen Hinterhöfen auf der Leine hängen.

● Las casas están precariamente construidas con  pedazos de cartón, restos de madera, chapas de zinc y madera prensada. Manchones de color les elevan de sus fundaciones charras. Residentes ingeniosos con iniciativa usan cualquier cosa que estaba tirada, donada e intercambiada, para mejorar y realizar sus lugares. Un sentido de respeto propio está siempre presente y se nota en la ropa recién lavada que cuelga en el fondo modesto para secarse en el sol.

● De manière précaire, les logements sont construits avec des morceaux de carton, de bois, de tôle ondulée et de panneau de particules récupérés. De généreuses taches de couleurs les édifient de ces fondations à bon marché. Faisant preuve d'initiative, les habitants utilisent tout ce qui a été abandonné, échangé ou donné pour améliorer, pour rehausser. Le sens de l'amour-propre est omniprésent, comme le témoigne d'ailleurs les vêtements sortant tout juste du lavage, suspendus dans la modeste arrière-cour.

Oil lamps, candles and torchlight illuminate the rooms in a gentle wash of magical light. For those who do not yet have electricity, as in days gone by, paraffin stoves will boil the kettle and candles will light the way.

Öllampen, Kerzen und Taschenlampe tauchen das Innere in ein magisches Licht. Für diejenigen, die noch keinen Strom haben, bringen Paraffinöfchen den Kessel zum Kochen und leuchten, wie in alten Tagen, Kerzen die Wege aus.

Lámparas de aceite, velas y antorchas iluminan los cuartos con una capa de luz suave. Para aquellos quienes todavía no tienen electricidad, como en los días de antaño, estufas de parafina hierven ollas, y velas iluminan el camino.

La lueur des lampes à pétrole, des bougies et des flambeaux baigne avec douceur les pièces d'une lumière merveilleuse. Ceux qui n'ont pas encore l'électricité mettent l'eau à bouillir, comme auparavant, sur des réchauds à paraffine, et s'éclairent à la bougie.

● Each room has its own décor of distinctive character and charm. Ingenious space saving methods are essential in the diminutive quarters.

Bicycles hang like massive mobiles above beds, beds become couches during the day.

● Jeder Raum hat sein eigenes Dekor mit unverwechselbarem Charakter und Charme. In diesen winzigen Quartieren muss jedes kleinste Stückchen Raum einfallsreich genutzt werden.

Fahrräder hängen wie Mobiles über dem Bett, Betten werden tagsüber zu Sofas.

● Cada cuarto tiene su propia decoración de carácter y encanto particular. Ingeniosos métodos para ahorrar espacio son esenciales en estos cuartitos chicos. Bicicletas suspendidas como juguetes colgantes sobre las camas, y camas se convierten en sofás durante el día.

● À chaque pièce son propre décor, au caractère et au charme distincts. L'utilisation de méthodes ingénieuses pour gagner de l'espace est essentielle dans ces tous petits domiciles : des bicyclettes sont suspendues telles des mobiles gigantesques au-dessus des lits, ces derniers devenant des divans pendant la journée.

● There exists a strong sense of community amongst the shack dwellers, a generosity beyond means, a fellowship of pride. With no official demarcation of land, neighbours must share a courtyard and be prepared to offer up any spare space if a new home needs to be erected.

● Unter den Bewohnern der Baracken besteht ein ausgeprägtes Gefühl der Zusammengehörigkeit, Großzügigkeit ohne Ende, eine Gemeinschaft des Stolzes. Ohne offizielle Parzellierung des Landes, teilen sich Nachbarn einen Hof und sind bereit jedes freie Stückchen Platz für die Errichtung einer neuen Unterkunft zu überlassen.

● Existe un gran sentido de comunidad entre los habitantes de los ranchos, una generosidad que va más allá de todo, una vecindad de orgullo. Sin demarcación oficial del terreno, los vecinos deben compartir un patio y estar dispuestos a ofrecer cualquier espacio libre, si un nuevo hogar necesita ser construido.

● Il existe parmi les habitants des bidonvilles, un fort esprit de communauté, une générosité hors pair, une fière camaraderie. Les parcelles de terre n'ayant pas de démarcation officielle, les voisins doivent donc se partager la même cour, et doivent se préparer à offrir tout espace libre, si besoin il y a de construire un nouveau logement.

● Vegetable patches and banana trees are carefully nurtured, usually b
the women and children of the community as the men are often awa
at work. For those living on the breadline, these crops go a long way t
feed their families.

● Kleine Gemüsebeete und Bananenstauden werden sorgfältig gepfleg
normalerweise von Frauen und Kindern der Gemeinschaft weil die Männe
oft auf der Arbeit sind. Für alle, die von einem Existenzminimum lebe
reicht der Ertrag, ihre Familie für eine gute Weile zu versorgen.

● Parcelas de vegetales y bananeros son cuidadosamente cultivados pc
las mujeres y niños de la vecindad, ya que los hombres a menudo está
fuera trabajando. Para ellos que apenas alcanzan a sobrevivir, estos cultivc
ayudan mucho en alimentar a sus familias.

● Des potagers et des bananiers sont cultivés soigneusement, d'habitud
par les femmes et les enfants de la communauté, car devant se rendr
au travail, les hommes sont souvent absents. Pour ceux vivant au seu
de la pauvreté, ces produits agricoles contribuent largement à nourr
leur famille.

The spirit in these humble surrounds is overwhelmingly joyous and welcoming. An exuberant throng of children eagerly awaits their turn on a round-a-bout in the village. Growing up with few material assets, it is more often the children's playful imaginations that will keep them occupied until their parents call them in for the evening meal.

In dieser einfachen Umgebung existiert ein überwiegend fröhlicher und freundlicher Geist. Eine ausgelassene Kinderschar in einer Siedlung alle wollen sie mal aufs Karussell. Ohne große materielle Gegenstände aufwachsend, ist es eher die spielerische Erfindungskraft der Kinder, die sie beschäftigt hält bis ihre Eltern sie zum Abendessen hereinrufen.

El espíritu en estos aledaños es sobrecogedor feliz y bienvenido. Una muchedumbre exuberante de niños entusiasmadamente esperando su turno sobre la glorieta en la aldea. Criándose con pocos bienes materiales, suele ser la imaginación juguetona de los niños que les mantiene ocupados hasta que los padres les llaman para cenar.

Dans ce cadre modeste, l'air est en très grande majorité, joyeux et accueillant. Un groupe d'enfants bouillonnants d'impatience attend son tour sur un manège du village. Grandissant avec peu de biens matériels, l'imagination enjouée des enfants les garderont souvent occupés jusqu'à que leurs parents les feront rentrer pour le repas du soir.

● An entrepreneurial temperament is ever burgeoning. An old beer crate and crudely cut chipboard become a makeshift table selling an assortment of sweets. A vintage sewing machine is the indispensable tool for a thriving sewing business.

● Überall keimt unternehmerisches Temperament auf. Ein alter Bierkasten und eine grob zugeschnittene Spanplatte werden zu einem Tisch, auf dem ein Sortiment von Süßigkeiten angeboten wird. Eine altehrwürdige Nähmaschine ist unentbehrlich für eine florierende Näherei.

● Un temperamento emprendedor siempre floreciendo. Un cajón viejo de cerveza y una tabla rudimentaria de madera prensada sirven como una mesa provisional para vender un surtido de caramelos. Una vieja máquina de coser de antaño, es una herramienta imprescindible para un negocio de costura próspero.

● L'esprit d'entreprise est en croissance permanente : une vieille caisse de bière et un panneau de particules mal coupé deviennent des tables de fortune sur lesquelles l'on vend toute une variété de bonbons ; une machine à coudre de l'époque devient l'outil indispensable dans une entreprise de couture florissante.

Vivid hues of sunshine and sky beckon customers to the local spaza shop.  Enjoy a Coca-Cola, have a mug of sweet tea, sit, chat and relax. Life is slow here, and away from the rat race of the cities, time beats to a mellow tune.

Sonnenschein und blauer Himmel verlocken zu einem Besuch des örtlichen Plaza-Ladens.  Sitzen, plaudern, sich bei einer Cola oder einem Becher mit süßem Tee entspannen.  Das Leben verläuft langsam hier, weitab vom Stress der Städte schlägt die Zeit ein gemächliches Tempo an.

Tonos de colores vivos de la luz del sol y del cielo llaman a clientes a la tienda local de "spaza". ¡Disfruta una Coca Cola, toma un tarro de té dulce, siéntate, charla, y descansa! La vida es lenta aquí, lejos de la vida febril de las ciudades, el tiempo marcha a un ritmo apacible.

Les vives nuances des rayons de soleil et du ciel attirent la clientèle vers le *spaza* du coin.  On y prend un coca, un mug de thé sucré, on s'assoit, on bavarde, on se détend…  Ici, la vie est au ralenti et, loin du rythme effréné des villes, le temps bat la mesure d'une douce mélodie.

- A vegetable shop of red, green and gold visually croons that laid-back reggae vibe. Bob Marley and Haile Selassi keep watch over the apples and bananas.

   Individuality abounds in these settlements and never ceases to captivate the imagination.

- Ein Gemüseladen mit Rot, Grün und Gold annonciert den lockeren Reggae-Rhythmus. Bob Marley und Haile Selassi wachen über Äpfel und Bananen.

   Alles in diesen Siedlungen ist voll Individualität und hört nicht auf die Sinne zu fesseln.

- Una tiendita de verduras de colores rojo, verde y amarillo, visualment tararea las vibras de reggae despreocupadas. Bob Marley y Haile Selas vigilan las manzanas y bananas.

   La individualidad abunda en estas poblaciones y nunca deja de cautiva la imaginación.

- Les tons rouges, verts et or des étalages du marchand de légume évoquent les sons décontractés d'une chanson de reggae. D'ailleurs, c a l'impression que Bob Marley et Hailé Sélassié surveillent les pommes les bananes…

   En effet, l'individualité abondante de ces bidonvilles ne cesse jamais captiver l'imagination.

Friendly faces and ubiquitous South African brands speak of familiarity and trust. Like many African communities, there is an allegiance to certain products that have been around for generations.

Freundliche Gesichter und allgegenwärtige südafrikanische Marken sprechen Bekanntsein und Vertrauen aus. Konsumenten in Afrika halten sich gern an Produkte, die schon eine lange Zeit auf dem Markt sind.

⬤ Caras simpáticas y productos de marca sudafricana siempre presentes hablan de familiaridad y confianza. Como en muchas comunidades africanas, hay una lealtad a ciertos productos que han sobrevivido por generaciones.

⬤ Des visages sympathiques et des marques de fabrique sud-africaines omniprésentes font allusion à ce qui est familier et auquel l'on peut faire confiance. Comme beaucoup de communautés africaines, l'on reste fidèle à certains produits qui existent depuis des générations.

● Braiding or shaving, salons in the sun are a familiar sight as locals keep abreast of the latest fashion trends. So sit down on an old beer crate and let the professionals make you look hip and happening!

● Flechten oder Rasieren, Freiluftsalons sind eine vertraute Erscheinung und stehen modisch voll im Trend. Platz nehmen, bitte, auf einer alten Bierkiste und lass dir einen professionellen Hip-Look verpassen.

● Trenzado o afeitado, salones de peluquería en el sol son una vista común mientras la vecindad se mantiene al día con la última moda. ¡Así siéntate sobre un cajón viejo de cerveza y deja que los profesionales te pongan de moda!

● Nattes, tête rasée… Les salons de coiffure en plein soleil offrent un spectacle familier, alors que les gens du quartier marchent avec leur temps selon les dernières tendances mode. En effet, pourquoi ne pas s'asseoir sur une vieille caisse de bière et se laisser créer une allure branchée par les professionnels du métier ?

Out here, even strangers are treated like family. Jovial voices holler greetings of a brand new and blessed day. Everywhere bright smiles echo the radiant sun. There exists a wonderful camaraderie that is sadly lost in exclusive suburbia.

Hier draußen werden sogar Fremde behandelt, als gehörten sie zur Familie. Grußworte verkünden mit jovialer Stimme einen neuen jungen und gesegneten Tag. Überall ein breites von der Sonne bestrahltes Lächeln auf den Gesichtern. Hier gibt es noch Formen der Kameradschaft, die in den exklusiven Vororten leider verloren gegangen sind.

Aquí, hasta extranjeros son tratados como familia. Voces felices vociferan saludos de un nuevo y bendito día. Por todos lados sonrisas amplias reflejan el sol radiante. Existe una camaradería que desafortunadamente no existe en las zonas residenciales exclusivas.

Ici, même les étrangers sont traités comme des membres de la famille. Des voix joviales crient le bonjour, évoquant une nouvelle et heureuse journée. Partout, de grands sourires font écho à un soleil radieux. Il y existe une camaraderie merveilleuse qui, malheureusement, dans l'exclusivité des banlieues, est perdue.

● A stockpile of second-hand bricks resting against a vividly coloured tin shack allude to the owner's dream of a solid brick house.

● Ein Vorrat von Backsteinen aus zweiter Hand, an eine leuchtend angemalte Wellblechbaracke gelehnt, deutet auf den Traum des Besitzers von einem soliden Backsteinhaus.

● Ladrillos de segunda mano almacenados contra un rancho de lata pintado con colores vivos, hacen alusiones a los sueños del dueño de tener una casa sólida de ladrillos.

● Un stock de briques d'occasion empilées contre une cabane en tôle aux couleurs éclatantes, fait allusion à la solide maison en brique dont rêve le propriétaire.

● Kaleidoscopic houses paint a vibrant picture on the dunes. Each and every shack is spontaneously unique. An unequivocal sign that cultural creativity is evolving with the times. As more and more formal housing is being built however, these animated structures will almost surely be a page in the history books of South Africa.

● Bunt wie in einem Kaleidoskop sind die Häuser in die Dünenlandschaft gestreut. Jede Baracke ist spontan entstanden und in ihrer Art einmalig. Ein Zeichen dafür, wie kulturelle Kreativität sich mit der Zeit entwickelt. Durch formell errichtete Behausungen ersetzt, werden diese lebendigen Strukturen schon bald in die Seiten der südafrikanischen Geschichtsbücher eingehen.

● Como un calidoscopio, las casas 'pintan' una vista exuberante sobre las dunas. Cada uno de los ranchos es único en su género. Sin duda e una muestra de que la creatividad cultural se desarrolla con los tiempo A medida que se construyen más y más casas formales, estas animada estructuras casi seguramente quedarán en las páginas de la histori de Sudáfrica.

● Des maisons kaléidoscopiques peignent une image vivante sur le dunes. Toutes les cabanes ont leur propre style spontané, indiquant san équivoque que la créativité culturelle évolue bien avec le temps. Comm de plus en plus de logements formels sont construits, ces structure animées rempliront sans doute un jour une page dans les livres d'histoir d'Afrique du Sud.

Murals of allegiance to a favourite soccer team, etchings and graffiti all serve to individualise the exteriors of the homes. Soccer is the most popular sport amongst black South Africans. Kaizer Chiefs and Orlando Pirates are teams that both hail from Soweto, and when they play against each other it is one of the most fanatical and popular soccer derbys worldwide. A stadium that seats 80 000 has been known to be filled with 95 000 frenzied fans.

Wandzeichnungen nennen favorisierte Fußballklubs, Skizzen und Graffiti geben dem Äußeren der Häuser individuellen Charakter. Fußball ist der populärste Sport unter den schwarzen Südafrikanern. Kaizer Chiefs und Orlando Pirates sind zwei Klubs aus Soweto, und ein Spiel der beiden gegeneinander zählt zu den weltweit fanatischsten und populärsten Begegnungen. Ein Stadium mit 80 000 Plätzen soll schon mal 95 000 verrückte Fans aufgenommen haben.

Murales que muestran lealtad a un equipo de fútbol favorito, grabados y graffiti, todo sirve para individualizar los exteriores de los hogares. El fútbol (soccer) es el deporte más popular entre los sudafricanos negros. Kaizer Chiefs y Orlando Pirates son los dos equipos que proceden de Soweto y cuando juegan uno contra el otro, es un de los más fanáticos y populares clásicos mundialmente. Un estadio de 80,000 asientos a veces se llena con más de 95,000 aficionados desenfrenados.

● Des muraux faisant allégeance à l'équipe de football préférée, des dessins gravés et des graffitis… enfin, tout sert à personnaliser l'extérieur des maisons. Le football est le sport le plus populaire parmi les Sud-Africains noirs. Les équipes de *Kaizer Chiefs* et d'*Orlando Pirates* proviennent toutes les deux de Soweto, et lorsque ces deux voisines s'affrontent, le match devient l'un des plus délirants et des plus populaires au monde. Cela c'est déjà vu qu'un stade de 80 000 places se remplisse de 95 000 fans en état de frénésie.

● Die Seele der Barackenstädte befindet sich oft in den örtlichen Kaschemmen – den beliebten Bars mit Musik, wo Bier, Schnaps und hausgebraute berauschende Getränke verkauft werden. In der Vergangenhe[.] entstand hier eine neue Kultur der Arbeiterklasse. Musikanten un[d] Kaschemmenwirte konnten sich dort über Wasser halten anstelle i[n] seelenlosen Minen oder Fabriken arbeiten zu müssen. Heutzutage könne[n] sich einige den Luxus eines Billardtisches leisten, in anderen amüsiert ma[n] sich beim Karten- oder Würfelspiel.

● El alma de los rancheríos se encuentra a menudo en los "shebeens" locales – cantinas populares donde tocan música y venden cerveza [y] bebidas intoxicantes caseras. En el pasado los "shebeens" ayudaban [a] crear una nueva cultura para la clase obrera; un método de supervivenc[ia] para músicos y "shebeen queens" (las anfitrionas de las tabernas) quiene[s] podían ganar un sueldo fijo en vez de ir a trabajar en una mina o en un[a] fábrica. Hoy en día algunas se dan el lujo de tener una mesa de bill[ar] mientras otras tienen clientes que juegan al dado y naipes.

● L'âme des bidonvilles se trouve souvent dans les shebeens du quartie[r] ces bars populaires, où l'on joue de la musique, et où l'on vend de [la] bière, de l'alcool et des brassages enivrants fait maison. Auparavant, l[es] shebeens assistèrent à la création d'une culture appartenant à une nouve[lle] classe ouvrière. Ces bars devinrent donc un moyen de survie pour l[es] musiciens et les « reines des shebeens » (les propriétaires d'auberge[s] qui vivaient alors de cet argent au lieu d'aller travailler dans des mines [ou] dans des usines. De nos jours, certains ont les moyens d'y installer un[e] table de billard américain, alors que d'autres voit la clientèle jouer aux d[és] ou aux cartes.

● The soul of the shanty towns is often to be found in the local shebeens – popular bars playing music and selling beer, liquor and intoxicating home-brews. In the past shebeens helped to create a new working-class culture. They became the method of survival for musicians and shebeen queens (tavern owners) who could rely on this money instead of going off to work in an ominous mine or a factory. These days some can afford the luxury of a pool table, while others see customers playing dice or cards.

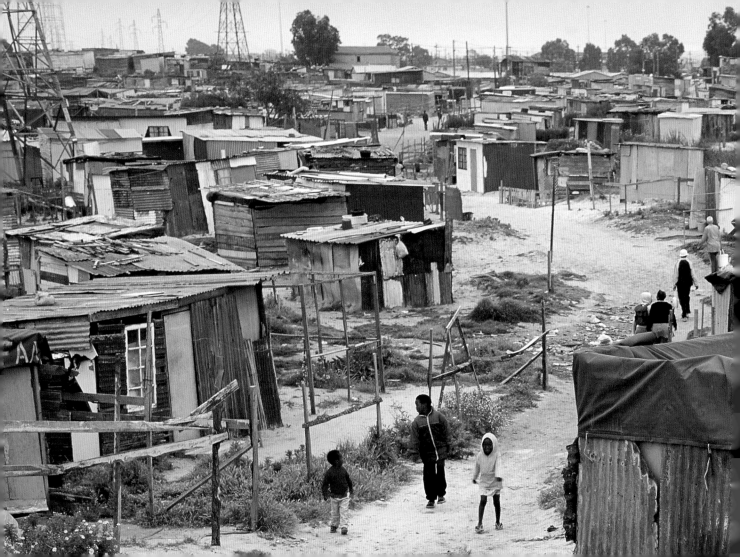

• Unlike the indigenous housing of the past of mud, wattle, sticks or branches, these informal settlements use leftover wooden planks, advertising boards, cardboard, corrugated iron, plastic, tarpaulins and chipboard.

• Anders als die traditionellen aus Lehm und Ästen errichteten Häuser, werden in den informellen Siedlungen überschüssige Holzplanken, Reklametafeln, Pappen, Wellblech, Plastik, Planen und Spanplatten verwendet.

• Históricamente las viviendas indígenas eran hechas de barro, zarzo, cañas y ramas pero hoy estas viviendas informales usan sobrantes de tablas de madera, vallas publicitarias, carteleras, cartón, chapas de zinc, plástico, lonas y madera prensada.

• Contrairement aux maisons d'autrefois, qui étaient elles construites en terre, avec du clayonnage, des bâtons ou des branches, ces logements informels comprennent des panneaux en bois, des panneaux d'affichage, du carton, de la tôle ondulée, de la matière plastique, des bâches, des panneaux de particules…

Guy Stubbs /africanpictures.net

● An overwhelming vivacity of spirit. A tangible feeling of pride. For al
their undeniable poverty, the people have found a content disposition that
money seldom buys, as these cheerful children with their ready smiles
attest to.

● Ein überwältigender Geist der Lebensfreude. Ein handfestes Gefühl vor
Stolz. Trotz nicht zu leugnender Armut besitzen die Menschen dennoch
eine Einstellung der Zufriedenheit, die mit Geld nicht zu bezahlen ist, und
was diese gutgelaunten Kinder mit stets bereitem Lächeln bezeugen.

● Un espíritu de vivacidad incontenible. Un sentido de orgullo palpable
A pesar de su innegable pobreza, el pueblo ha encontrado una satisfacción
que muy pocas veces el dinero puede comprar, como lo demuestran esto
niños alegres con sus amplias risas.

● Un esprit débordant de vitalité. Une sensation de fierté tangible
Malgré leur pauvreté incontestable, ces gens ont pourtant trouvé un
manière d'être qui ne s'achète que rarement, comme en font preuve ce
enfants joyeux au sourire facile.

● A lightening streak of liquid yellow and orange rages through the sleepy shacks. Very few people have their own transport and therefore rely on the public trains and buses or the privately owned mini-bus taxis.

● Ein Blitzstrahl von flüssigem Gelb und Orange saust durch die verschlafene Barackensiedlung. Nur wenige haben ihr eigenes Transportmittel und sind daher auf die öffentlichen wie Bahn und Bus oder die von privater Hand betriebenen Minibus-Taxis angewiesen.

● Como un rayo  líquido de luz rojo y amarillo, el tren zumba por entre las chozas dormilonas.  Muy poca gente tiene su propio transporte y así debe contar con trenes y autobuses públicos o mini-bus taxis privados.

● Un éclair strié de jaune et d'orange fluides passe avec fureur parmi les cabanes à peine réveillées. Très peu d'entre eux ayant leur propre moyen de transport, les gens dépendent donc des transports en commun : trains, bus et taxis minibus, ces derniers appartenant à des propriétaires privés.

Flamboyant in colour as it is ebullient in sound. With an ever-thumping ethnic beat, the mini-bus taxis squeeze in hoards of commuters and transport them to and from work.

Prächtig in der Farbe, übersprudelnd im Sound mit mächtig-dumpfem Afrika Beat transportieren die Minibus-Taxis Tausende von Pendlern.

Exuberante de color como efervescente en sonido. Con un estallado ritmo constante, el mini-bus apiña un montón de pasajeros y los transporta de ida y vuelta a su trabajo.

Leur couleur est aussi flamboyante que leur sonorité est exubérante, avec un rythme ethnique constant, les taxis minibus transportent des passagers entassés, faisant tous les jours la navette entre leur domicile et leur lieu de travail.

● Typical of a developing country, the black African population has a relatively large percentage of children under the age of fifteen years old – almost a third of the population. The camaraderie between these kids, on the streets and in their playgrounds, is tangible.

● Der Anteil an Kindern unter 15 Jahren in der schwarzafrikanischer Bevölkerung ist, wie in anderen Entwicklungsländern, relativ hoch – fast ein Drittel der Gesamtbevölkerung. Die Kameradschaft unter diesen Kinderr auf der Straße und den Spielplätzen ist greifbar.

● Típico de un país subdesarrollado, la población del africano negro tiene un porcentaje bastante alto de niños de menos de quince años – casi la tercera parte de la población. La camaradería entre estos niños en las calles y en los espacios de recreo, es palpable.

● Comme l'est typique des pays en voie de développement, la population africaine noire connait un pourcentage relativement élevé d'enfant au-dessous de l'âge de quinze ans, soit presque un tiers de la population. Dans les rues et dans les cours de récréation, ces gosses font preuve d'une camaraderie palpable.

• A sprawling sea of settlements. Imaginative names of these towns include Barcelona; Boys Town; Happy Valley; Bhambay; Tambo Square; Crossroads; Vietnam and Sweet Home.

• Eine ausufernde Siedlung. Zu den einfallsreichen Namen dieser Townships gehören: Barcelona, Boys Town, Happy Valley, Bhambay, Tambo Square, Crossroads, Vietnam und Sweet Home.

• Un descontrolado mar de villas miserias. Nombres llamativos de estos lugares incluyen Barcelona, Aldea de los Muchachos, Valle Feliz, Bombay, Plaza de Tambo, Encrucijada, Vietnam y Hogar Dulce.

• Une mer d'habitations s'étale. Parmi les noms pleins d'imagination de ces communes figurent : *Barcelone, « Boys Town »* (nom d'un foyer pour garçons), *la vallée du Bonheur, Bhambay, la place Tambo, le Carrefour, Viêt-nam* et *« Sweet Home »*.

A hot sweet mug of coffee on a chilly winter morning. A typical breakfast would also include hot mealie meal porridge – a staple product of South Africa.

Eine Tasse heißen süßen Kaffees an einem frostigen Wintermorgen. Zu nem typischen Frühstück gehört auch ein heißer Maisbrei – eines der rundnahrungsmittel in Südafrika.

Un tarro de café dulce en una madrugada fría. Un desayuno típico incluiría papilla de maíz caliente, un alimento básico de Sudáfrica.

Un froid matin d'hiver, l'on boit un mug de café chaud et sucré. Un petit-déjeuner typique comprend également une bouillie chaude de farine de maïs, produit de base en Afrique du Sud.

An eclectic mix of pastels and brights, iron and cardboard, home to these
vo brothers and siblings playing with a wire toy car.

Eine kunterbunte Mixtur von Pastell- und hellen Farben, Eisen und
appe – das Zuhause dieser zwei Brüder und Geschwister, beim Spiel mit
nem Drahtauto.

● Una mezcla ecléctica de colores suaves y brillantes, de hierro y cartón,
es el hogar de este grupo de hermanos jugando con un típico cochecito
hecho de alambre.

● L'habitation de ces deux frères d'une même fratrie, s'amusant avec une
petite voiture en fil de fer, est un mélange éclectique de tons pastel et de
couleurs vives, de ferraille et de carton…

A young boy enjoys a quiet moment in the setting sun on the doorstep of his home.

On the surface, these dwellings certainly have no remarkable architectural value, but beyond that, they are spiritual abodes, places of refuge, conversation, the warmth of kindred spirits.

Ein Junge in der Stille der untergehenden Sonne vor seiner Hütte.

Oberflächlich betrachtet haben diese Unterkünfte keinen besonderen architektonischen Wert, sind aber spirituelle Heimstätten, Stätten der Zuflucht, der Gespräche, der Wärme und Nähe zu gleichgesinnten Menschen.

Un muchachito disfruta un momento tranquilo al atardecer, en el umbral de su casa.

Superficialmente estas viviendas ciertamente no tienen un valor arquitectónicamente notable, pero más allá, son domicilios del alma, lugares de refugio, conversación, con el calor de almas gemelas.

Un jeune garçon apprécie un moment de tranquillité au soleil couchant devant la porte de sa maison.

À première vue, ces habitations n'ont certainement aucune grande valeur architecturale, or, au-delà de tout cela, elles sont des demeures spirituelles, des lieux de refuge, de conversation, où l'on ressent la chaleur de l'âme sœur.

● While most homes have relied on paraffin lamps, oil or gas more and more have been blessed with the convenience of electricity. Power lines zigzag in a disorderly fashion, bringing the accessibility that most modern homes take for granted. Television, refrigeration, light, hot water and telephones.

● Während die meisten Häuser sich mit Paraffinlampen, Öl oder Gas zufrieden geben müssen, kommen immer mehr in den Genuss der Elektrizität. Stromkabel ziehen sich ohne besondere Ordnung im Zickzack über das Gelände und machen das zugänglich, was in modernen Häusern selbstverständlich ist - Fernseher, Kühlschrank, Licht, heißes Wasser und Telefon.

● Mientras que la mayoría de los hogares usan lámparas de parafina, gas o aceite, más y más han sido privilegiados con la comodidad de la electricidad. Cables de alta tensión zigzag en un modo desordenado. Trayendo consigo el acceso fácil que la mayoría de las casas modernas toman como algo normal. Televisión, heladeras, luz, agua caliente y teléfonos.

● Alors que la plupart des foyers dépendent de lampes à pétrole, de l'huile de paraffine et du gaz, de plus en plus d'entre eux ont la chance de disposer du confort de l'électricité. Des lignes à haute tension font des zigzags de façon désordonnée, donnant l'accès à la télévision, réfrigération, l'électricité, l'eau chaude et le téléphone, choses sur lesquelles comptent la majorité des foyers modernes.

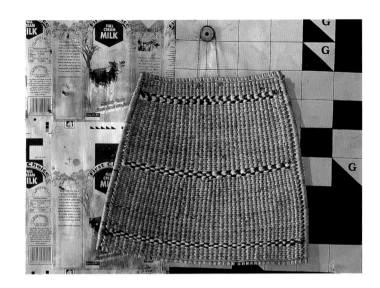

House-proud. With a shortage of money comes an abundance of ingenuity. Packaging over-runs have been used as wallpaper in a riot of pattern and colour. A straw bag becomes a decorative wall hanging. The rest of the country is sitting up and taking notice and some upmarket décor shops have emulated these fresh ideas.

Besitzerstolz. Wo nicht viel Geld vorhanden ist, muss die Fantasie nachhelfen. Verpackungsüberschuss wird als Tapete verwendet mit einem Karneval von Formen und Farben. Eine Strohtasche hängt dekorativ an der Wand. Der Rest des Landes horcht auf und vornehme Inneneinrichtungsgeschäfte haben sich bereits von diesen frischen Ideen inspirieren lassen.

Meticuloso. Con poco dinero viene una abundancia de ingeniosidad inventiva. Sobrantes de envolturas han sido usados para empapelar paredes en una profusión de dibujos estampados y colores. Una bolsa de paja se convierte en una decoración colgada en la pared. El resto del país está tomando nota y algunas tiendas de categoría están copiando estas ideas nuevas.

Tout est impeccable chez elle. Avec le manque de moyens, l'ingéniosité abonde. Le surplus des emballages tapisse les murs dans une débauche de motifs et de couleurs. Un sac en paille accroché au mur donne un aspect décoratif. D'ailleurs, le reste du pays est en train de réagir et des magasins de décoration haut de gamme auraient même imité ces idées neuves.

It may seem incongruous, but street numbers identify the houses so that post may be delivered to their doors. Whether you're visiting a family home, or an international tourist resting at one of the growing numbers of B&B's in these colourful informal settlements, the doors will always open welcomingly.

Es mag paradox klingen, aber Straßennummern identifizieren die Unterkünfte, so dass Postzustellung möglich ist. Ob man nun eine dieser Familienunterkünfte besucht oder in diesen informellen Siedlungen als Tourist in einer der zunehmenden Zahl von Unterkünften mit Bett und Frühstück übernachtet - die Türen werden jederzeit gastfreundschaftlich geöffnet.

Tal vez parece extraño pero los números identifican las casas para que el correo pueda ser entregado en las puertas correctas. Si está visitando una familia, o es un turista internacional alojándose en una de las pensiones, sus puertas siempre se abrirán con una cordial bienvenida.

Cela pourrait sembler incongru, mais des numéros identifient ces maisons pour que le courrier puisse être livré à leur porte. Que vous soyez en visite dans une maison de famille, ou que vous soyez un touriste international logeant dans une des nombreuses maisons d'hôte dont le nombre ne fait qu'accroître au sein de ces communes informelles, les portes vous seront toujours ouvertes pour vous accueillir.

Eric Miller /africanpictures.net

● A dazzling washing detergent billboard. A boldness of blazing colour. The lustre of light-reflecting surfaces. Shanty towns are alive with an almost surreal illumination. But it is the beauty of the people that ultimately shines through.

On dry and derelict plains, in the ugly face of poverty, these individuals can still hold up their heads in dignity and pride. They've overcome arduous obstacles and turned everything around to show the world a rare and imaginative beauty – their homes, their shanty towns.

● Eine grelle Reklametafel für ein Waschmittel. Die Bravour leuchtender Farben. Der Glanz reflektierender Oberflächen. Barackenstädte sind in ihrer Lebendigkeit fast surreal erhellt. Schließlich aber ist es die Schönheit der Menschen, was durchscheint.

Auf trockenen und verfallenen Ebenen, unschöne Armut vor Augen, tragen diese Menschen hier ihren Kopf hoch in Würde und Stolz. Sie haben gelernt, schwierigste Hindernisse zu überwinden, haben alles zu ihrem Vorteil gewendet und können nun der Welt eine seltene und phantasievolle Schönheit zeigen – ihr Zuhause, ihre Barackenstädte.

● Una cartelera llamativa de detergente. La fuerza de color resplandeciente. El brillo de superficies reflejándose. Los rancheríos se alegran con una iluminación casi surrealista. Pero es la belleza del pueblo que se nota más.

Sobre las llanuras marginadas y polvorientas, la cara fea de la pobreza, estas personas todavía pueden levantar sus cabezas con dignidad y orgullo. Han superado obstáculos duros y han dado vuelta a todo para mostrar al mundo una belleza imaginativa y diferente – sus hogares, sus barriadas.

● Un panneau éblouissant affichant un détergent de lessive. Un flamboiement de couleurs vigoureuses. Des surfaces lustrées où la lumière se reflète. Une illumination presque surréaliste anime les bidonvilles. Au final cependant, c'est la beauté rayonnante de ces gens qui transparaît.

Sur des plaines sèches et abandonnées, face à une pauvreté détestable, ces individus peuvent néanmoins regarder le monde en face avec dignité et fierté. Car, ayant surmonté des obstacles ardus, ils ont réussi à faire tout d'un rien, pour révéler au monde une esthétique peu commune et pleine d'imagination : celle de leur maison, de leur bidonville.

Jodi Bieber - South Photographs /africanpictures.net

● Photographers: ● Photographen: ● Fotógrafos: ● Photographes :
Gcinumuzi Ndwalane - pg 6-7, 9-13, 24-25, 27, 32-35, 42, 44, 47, 5?
56-57, 59
Neil Austen - pg 1, 4, 16-17, 21, 31, 36-39, 43, 46, 48, 52, 58, 60-61
John Hone - pg 2, 22, 41

● Other contributions by: ● Andere Beiträge von:
● Otras contribuciones por:- ● Autres contributions par :
Jodi Bieber - South Photographs /africanpictures.net - pg 63, 64
David Larsen - The Media Bank /africanpictures.net - pg 14
Cedric Nunn /africanpictures.net - pg 18
Eric Miller /africanpictures.net - pg 50, 62
Guy Stubbs /africanpictures.net - pg 26, 28, 40, 54

### Art Publishers (Pty) Ltd
*Durban, Johannesburg, Cape Town*